Recollections Of
An Amish Childhood

Recollections Of An Amish Childhood

52 Poems, Lyrics, & Essays

Indiana Writer & Poet
Moses L. Hochstetler

Copyright © 2009 by Moses L. Hochstetler.

First edition—December, 2009

Poem & Essay Copyrights © 1990-2009

ISBN: Hardcover   978-1-4415-8677-3
             Softcover   978-1-4415-8676-6

All rights reserved. No part of this book may be reproduced or transmitted in any form or by any means, electronic or mechanical, including photocopying, recording, or by any information storage and retrieval system, without permission in writing from the copyright owner.

This book was printed in the United States of America.

Cover:

Pre-school picture
of Poet Moses L. Hochstetler
with 2 older brothers

To order additional copies of this book, contact:
Xlibris Corporation
1-888-795-4274
www.Xlibris.com
Orders@Xlibris.com
69540

CONTENTS

Poems:

Little Seeds	1
A Fruitful Yield	2
Way Back When	3
Huskin' Corn	4
The Children Learned to Work Hard	5
Out On the Farm	6
Mammas Kitchen Threshing Day	7
Under the Lilac Bush	8
Rural Charm	10
Whispers of the U-Creek	12
The Old Wood-Stove	13
The Red Brick House	14
Heaven On Earth	15
Ode To An Ancient Spiel	16
Beauty Still Lingers	17
Home In Kosciusko	18
"Dad"	20
Mother's Love	22
Old Man Winter	23
I Dream Of Yesterday	24
Fleeting Youth	26
I Dreamed of Home Again last Night	27
Sparkling Good Morning	28
Kindred Memories	29
January Sixth	30
Rainbow	32
Sonnet of Peace	33
Scarecrow	34
The Outhouse Out Back	35
Our Work Is Not Done Yet	36
Shorty, a Horse of a Different Color	37
Aunt Matildy's Soup	38

When Rosie O'Riley Cleans the House 40
Wonder In Their Eyes 42
When the Geese Fly By 44
Welcome! 45
Shadows of the Grave 46
A View From My Window 47

Lyrics:

Beauty Around Us 48
The Lilacs Are Blooming 49
Corn Pone and Rivel Soup 50

Essays:

Maple Syrup Season 52
Shocking Wheat and Oats 54
Threshing Day 56
Putting Hay Away 58
Making Apple Butter 60
Butchering Day 62
Amish Weddings 64
Amish Recreation 66
Amish "Frolics" 68
Making Ice Cream 69
Childhood Memories 70

"Little Seeds" won first place for me in a contest sponsored by Cader Publishing of Troy, Michigan. This is one of my earlier poems, and expresses my fondness for the kindness and wonderful family life shown me, and experienced by many of those raised in an Amish home.

Little Seeds

In the heart are etched the memories
Of golden moments past:
Of soft and gentle spoken words
And praise upon us cast,
Endearing smiles and helpful hands
Which often held our own;
The little seeds of selfless deeds
That long ago were sown.

In the heart are etched the memories
Of golden moments past:
Of lips that kissed away the tears
And hugs that held us fast,
Of warm and tender loving care
And sacrifices made;
The little seeds of selfless deeds
That grow while others fade.

In the heart are etched the memories
Of golden moments past,
Sweet memories that linger on;
As diamonds do they last.
A mother and a father's gift
Of time, in times of old;
The little seeds of selfless deeds
That shine as polished gold.

By age eight I was already sitting behind a 3-horse hitch helping with the plowing, preparing the soil, and helping out my 10 older brothers and 3 older sisters husk the many acres of corn. "A Fruitful Yield" expresses the busy but carefree life experienced at home on the farm, and compares the "fruitful yield" with the growth and development of the family. This poem was at one time published in Successful Farming Magazine.

A Fruitful Yield

The Little boy walked on the soil and clay,
His bare feet warm with the heat of the day.
All around him was the fresh plowed field,
And you needn't wait long for a fruitful yield.

The little boy stood midst the newly planted corn,
His shirt was all tattered and his pants were torn;
But he didn't miss all the worldly wealth,
The boy on the farm had abundant health.

The little boy ran among the corn stalks high,
A song in his heart and never a sigh;
Happy as a lark in the tall corn field,
And you needn't wait long for a fruitful yield.

The little boy helped on the harvest day;
Plucking and shucking and picking that-a-way.
The corn piled high in the wagon box
And the bins on the farm were bulging at the locks.

The little boy is grown now and misses the farm;
His wife and his children standing at his arm,
And his children are growing like the weeds of the field
And you needn't wait long for a fruitful yield.

"Way Back When" makes me sound older than I really am. Actually, this poem was written so that it could be taken both ways by the reader: (1) Back when I lived among the Amish, or (2) back in the time before the automobile when everyone lived in the "horse and buggy" days.

Way Back When

I remember way back when
The horses pulled the plow,
And it wasn't automation that
Would milk the Guernsey cow;
The chicken house was big enough
To hold a dozen hens,
And we had a lot of money if
We had some fives and tens.

I remember way back when
The husband and the wife,
Would really mean forever when
They tied the knot for life;
The mother was the mother and
The children knew their place,
And the father would come home at night
To say the table grace.

This poem pretty much explains itself. Modern conveniences have their benefits, but as a rule, family activities and close knit family ties are not among them.

Huskin' Corn

They have those pickers now-a-days
Can pick eight rows at once;
In an hour they can pick more corn
Than we picked in a month.
And I remember years ago
We picked from early morn;
The fun we had a-huskin' it,
Why, 't was worth more than the corn!
The whole family'd go a-huskin';
We'd have a good old time,
A-tellin' jokes and spinnin' yarns
And recitin' little rhymes.
Today the family's breakin' up
And driftin' all apart.
I think part of the problem is
We've gotten way too smart.
Perhaps we should slow down a bit
Just like the good old days,
With whole families huskin' corn
And forget how much it pays!

Like "Huskin' Corn" all the farm chores that inspired "The Children Learned To Work Hard" demanded that the whole family work together to get the job done. These activities taught cooperation and responsibility on the part of every family member; something that children cannot learn through video games and rock music.

The Children Learned to Work Hard

When at home with Mom and Dad on the farm back years ago,
We'd mow and rake the clover hay to form a neat windrow,
And we'd hope for sunny weather and the wind to dry the leaves,
Then we'd stash the hay in hay lofts to well beyond the eaves.
Though my muscles hurt and quivered from the lifting of the bales,
And the hard and brittle stems scratched and broke my finger nails;
Though I'd rather have been playing or just resting on a cot;
The children learned to work hard, and that was worth a lot!

In the hottest days of summer with a coat of chaff and dust,
With sweat just pouring off my face, and off my neck and bust,
Dad would drive his team of horses through the fields of ripened wheat,
With the binder cutting bundles in that all-consuming heat,
While the rest of us would shock it from the dawn till moon was bright,
And if luck was any comfort it would take but half the night.
Though the task would make me weary and the day was humid hot;
The children learned to work hard, and that was worth a lot!

My dad had lots of cows to milk, and heifers, hogs, and hens,
And that meant early chores to do with late nights cleaning pens.
My mom did all her gardening and canned her peas and corn,
Idleness was viewed by her with unrelenting scorn.
The weeds all needed plucking out, the berries gathered in;
How my back would ache with pain and blisters break my skin!
Yes, we all had work to do, And may I ask for what?
The children learned to work hard, and that was worth a lot!

MOSES L. HOCHSTETLER

Farm life has many benefits other than the monetary profits that can be gleaned. While the Amish did not use tractors when I was raised among them, there were many farmers living around them who did. This poem reflects on those memories.

Out On the Farm

A house with lots of shade trees,
To cool the heat of day;
A silo full of chopped corn,
A barn, alfalfa hay.

A man upon a tractor,
A plow that turns the sod;
A disk and a harrow
Breaking every clod.

A cow that's good for milking,
A steer for meat, a hog;
Some laying hens, a horse or two,
A black and white dog.

Fields and fields of fallow ground,
The barren fields reborn;
Farmers in the afternoon
Cultivating corn.

Paid holidays, pension plans,
And raises guaranteed?
No! And no vacations
When there are cows to feed!

Planting time and harvest time,
And work that's never done;
Undoubtedly a pleasant job
For wages next to none.

Threshing day was an exciting time which all the young Amish children anticipated. Neighbors with their wagons and teams of horses would come from miles around to participate. The threshing rig came chugging into the drive to set up by the barn. There were always huge full course meals laid out for the hard working crew. "Tae" is the Amish word for tea.

Mammas Kitchen Threshing Day

Threshing wheat on threshing day,
Men on wagons come our way;
Put on a pan, put on a pot,
Stoke the coals up mighty hot!

Boil the noodles, boil the beef,
Make the salad leaf by leaf,
"Devil them eggs" is what they say;
Mamma's kitchen threshing day.

Cooking corn and cooking peas,
Slicing bread and slicing cheese;
Aromatic'ly okay,
Mamma's kitchen threshing day.

Baking cake and baking pie;
Apple, pumpkin and shoefly;
Still can smell that spearmint tae,
Mamma's kitchen threshing day!

At the northwest corner of our red brick house, right next to the big wind mill, grew a giant cluster of lilacs. During the summer months, taking cover underneath its drooping thick shaded branches was one of my favorite cool places to hang out.

Under the Lilac Bush

Ah, the scent of lilacs blooming,
How it brings forth joyful tears,
How it stirs up youthful memories
Of the long gone yesteryears,
Of a bush of lilacs thriving
Plush and thick in our front lawn,
Intertwining branches growing
Ever shading on and on.
All the scented flowers sprinkled
In profusion 'mongst the leaves,
With its mystical illusion
Of the tapestry it weaves,
In a purple greenish pattern
As a covering for my den;
My perfumed Shangrila
That I would visit now and then.

'T was a welcome place and hideout
From all troubling kith and kin,
Where I could make my peace with heaven
And could make my peace within;
In that sanctuary lilac
With its branch encircling wreath,
Giving comfort, peace and solace
From its refuge underneath.

Often I would take my troubles
And my childish grief and pain
To that haven 'neath the lilacs,
Both in sunshine and in rain.
There my pensive brow would soften,
There my aches would fade away,
There my tear-eyed face would brighten
In the coolest shade of day.

My dear mother heavy laden
With her worries and her cares,
Would so quickly smile with pleasure
When I plucked the flowers there,
And I'd bunch them all together
In a wild abandoned way,
For the sight of lilacs blooming
Would soon melt her frowns away;
And though I'm grown now, and older,
Yet my griefs can't be denied,
And with heaviness the burdens
I have often heaped inside;
Until I think of shaded lilacs
Plush and thick upon the lawn,
Intertwining branches growing,
Ever shading on and on.

Those who, as a youth, have had the opportunity to spend time on a farm will be able to relate to this poem.

Rural Charm

Have you ever spent a summer;
Lazy summer on a farm?
With the cats and little kittens,
With the horses and their fittin's,
With the cattle and the calves out in the barn?

Have you heard the rooster crowing;
Loudly crowing come the dawn?
Have you seen the misty sunrise,
Pink and gold before your two eyes;
Shine in glory twixt the trees out in the lawn?

Have you ever trampled barefoot;
Reckless barefoot in the clay?
In the fresh-plowed dirt and diggin's;
On the clods, both small and big 'nes
Till they crumbled 'round your toes so cool and gray?

Have you played upon a hay-mow;
Pungent haymow way up high?
Have you jumped and rolled and tumbled,
With your friends together jumbled
Till you laughed so hard you 'most commenced to cry?

Have you romped on country acres;
Country acres in the sun?
Have you waded knee-deep streams
Splashing cool as in your dreams,
Then went dipping with your clothes off just for fun?

Have you ever spent a summer;
Busy summer on a farm?
Chased a rat or chased a mouse;
Flushed a pheasant or a grouse,
And experienced rural living with its charm?

Having more than 100 acres to roam around on as a child, with a creek running in and out of the farm in the shape of a "U" has its advantages. Memories of this care free time on the farm inspired this poem.

Whispers of the U-Creek

In the evening when the shadows dull
The harsh and glaring stress of the day;
When pillows melt the tensions away,
My heart steals back to an early age:

Back to the meadows where the U-Creek
Does softly whisper yesterday's words
Of carefree times and grazing herds,
Of barefoot boys and purple sage;

Back to meadows where the butterflies
Come back to taunt a ten-year-old,
Where bumblebees in their search of gold
Go wending through the timothy;

Back to a time when the summer months
Are filled with crickets and killdeer,
And the U-creek whispers into my ear
"Come back to me, come back to me."

Having a fireplace is nice, but the next best thing is having a coal or a wood-burning stove for the family to gather around during those cold winter evenings.

The Old Wood-Stove

I remember the days as a child I reclined
On a rocker beside the old stove;
That welcome old stove on the living-room floor,
That wood-burning, coal-burning, cast-iron stove
That crackled with fire in the pit of its core
With a savory smoke that I still can smell now,
Escaping from out of that cavernous door.

When the winters were cold and they cut to the quick,
And I shivered outside in the snow;
My fingers were numb and my swollen feet blue
In that nose-freezing, toes-freezing, cold-as-ice snow.
It didn't take long to know just what to do:
Find a comforting place right next to that stove
With its fire belching smoke up the hot chimney flue.

So delightfully warm was that wood-burning stove,
So cheerful a place we could meet;
That welcoming stove on the living-room floor,
That heart-warming, soul-warming, bastion of heat,
That crackled with fire, that blazed with a roar,
From the red and orange flames of the logs and the coal
Flickering so bright through the eisenglass door.

And we all sat around that old living-room stove
Eating things that would just hit the spot,
While cold on the outside the winter winds blew,
That round-bellied, pot-bellied stove stayed hot,
And kept us all cozy and warm through and through,
As it sang us a song of a tropical breeze
To the tune of that wind-blown old chimney flue.

My parents, ten brothers, and three of my sisters (all older) and I, all lived together in a five bedroom red brick house. It was not a big house, and had none of the modern conveniences, but we made do, with room to spare for occasional guests. I have nothing but fond memories of this wonderful house and home, including the huge dining table, where all fourteen of us children, including Mom and Dad, had our special places to sit.

The Red Brick House

The red brick house with the circular drive
Will always be home to me.
Surrounded by maples and spacious green lawn,
With song birds to wake me at breaking of dawn.
Lavender lilacs and flowers in bloom;
Fit for a princess; fit for her groom.
The red brick house with the circular drive
Forever my home will be.

The red brick house with the circular drive
Where loving hands cared for me.
Surrounded by brothers and sisters within,
A family including the cousins and kin,
Where welcome guest could find table spread wide;
Fit for a prince and fit for his bride.
The red brick house with the circular drive
Forever my home will be.

The red brick house with the circular drive
Only in mind's eye to see.
Though bricks are now broken and house is no more,
My roots are still there, just inside the door,
Where family shared love to make the heart sing;
Fit for a queen and fit for a king.
The red brick house with the circular drive
Forever my home will be.

This poem expresses just a few of the pleasantries I experienced as a child growing up on the farm. While all of these nature delights may not be experienced simultaneously, they can all be experienced in their seasons.

Heaven On Earth

Peach trees and pear trees,
Ripe sugar-plums;
Garden's aglow with
Asters and mums.

Lilacs and roses,
White thistledown;
Dandelions sprouting
An amber-gold crown.

Crickets in clover,
Green katydids;
Bees making honey,
Goats nursing kids.

Finches and warblers,
Swallows and more
Feathered wings riding
The wind as they soar.

Butterflies dancing
Above the grape vine;
Whippoorwill calling
His mate in the pine.

All about there is
Life and new birth;
Which part is heaven,
And which part is earth?

I was always fascinated by the activities going on in our local blacksmith shop. It seems our horse-drawn farm implements were forever breaking down and in need of repair. This poem attempts to capture the sights and sounds of the blacksmith shop; practicing an art almost as old as man himself.

Ode To An Ancient Spiel

The sputter and spit of the fiery pit
With a snarling flame of red,
As the hot coals glow
From the bellows that blow
In the blacksmith's humble shed.

A-rat-a-tat-tat, a-rat-a-tat-tat,
A-rink-a-dink-dink ado;
Is the sound that is heard
With never a word
For the likes of me or you.

The hiss of a cat from the water vat
As the iron cools to blue:
The steam and the smoke,
The grate and the poke,
The soot of the chimney flue.

The sweltering heat and the rhythmic beat,
The shower of sparkling steel;
The clash and clamor
Of anvil and hammer—
An ode to an ancient spiel.

The "Red Brick House" where I grew up was torn down, and a new house built in its place, but this poem wasn't inspired as much by my old home as by some of the neighborhood houses that were allowed to deteriorate.

Beauty Still Lingers

The house is decrepit,
The roof full of holes;
The windows are broken,
The lawn creased by moles.

The sidewalks are crumbling,
The barn in decay;
What once was a home,
Is no home today.

But beauty still lingers
Out front by the trees;
Among the azaleas
And pink peonies.

My father's 120 acre dairy farm was situated in the northwest corner of Kosciusko county in Indiana. It was a serene setting with maples and pines in our front yard; our garden, truck patch, and orchard to the south, our barn to the north of the house, and the "U-Creek" running just to the north of the barn. Our farm stretched to the east for half a mile, and our 10 acres of woods bordered the eastern end of the farm.

Home In Kosciusko

In Kosciusko County
Was a house of brick and wood,
There beside a well of water
Where there once a windmill stood;
Where the lilacs bloomed in springtime,
Where the crimson clover grew,
And the twining morning glories
Sparkled with the diamond dew.

There just off of road One Hundred,
South of Federal Highway Six,
On one hundred twenty acres,
With the horses, cows, and chicks;
There I grew from early childhood
To my later upper teens,
There I witnessed charm and beauty
In those glorious rural scenes.

There the gold finch and the robin
Made their home and kept their guard,
And the wren would build her nest
Out in the grape vines of our yard.
There the hawks would hunt for rodents,
And the martins soared the sky,
There the hoot owls kept their vigil
On their night posts from on high.

There I saw the U-creek meander
Through the early corn and wheat,
There I saw the maple growing,
Giving shade from summer heat;
There I saw the autumn colors,
The migration of the goose,
And I saw the winter snow
Clinging to the Norway spruce.

Just south of that old house
Was a lovely garden plot;
Where the radishes and lettuce
Grew beside the flowered spot;
Where we'd pick the peas and beans
And we'd dig potatoes out,
Where the children learned production
And what work was all about.

There my father and my mother
Raised all fourteen of their brood,
And it couldn't have been easy,
For it took a lot of food;
Back home in Kosciusko,
In that house of brick and wood—
In a home where both the parents
Did the best that parents could.

Even though his very demeanor demanded respect and honor, My father was a very lovable and jovial individual. He worked hard to provide for his large family, and succeeded in more ways than one.

"Dad"

It was just a short while ago, Dad,
That we worked and we played by your side;
But the days, the months, the years sped by
As time cannot be denied.
For the shadows of day would grow long, Dad,
And the sun would sink low in the west;
And the cold winter winds would blow, Dad,
And the birds take leave of their nest.

It's not just the hard work you did, Dad,
Through the heat of the day for us all,
And it's not just the things you gave us:
Winter, spring, summer, and fall.
It's the way you shared of your life, Dad,
With the loss of your sleep and your rest.
And it's the way you handled yourself, Dad,
When the rest of us weren't at our best.

It is not just the harvest of grain, Dad,
But the planting and care of the seed;
And it's not just the way you would scold us
Whenever we wouldn't heed—
It's the way that you felt of our pain, Dad;
From the harm in the things that we'd do.
It's the way you belonged to us, Dad,
It's the way we belonged to you.

All the times you suffered for us, Dad,
While you gave us the cheer of your song;
And now that you're no longer with us,
It seems that we often long
For the time we can see you again, Dad,
And to hear you laugh as we meet;
To talk of the times gone by, Dad,
As we sit at the table and eat.

My mother was a hard-working, quiet, unassuming, and unpretentious type of person, and I never heard her argue with my father. She never showed favoritism to any of her 14 children, and she did all she could to provide us with a comfortable and clean home. She loved each of us, and we all loved her in return.

Mother's Love

No other memories endure the test of time
To fill with such abiding fondness still,
As the memories of Mother's love sublime;
May she rest in quiet peace upon the hill.

Until the sound of trumpets blasting rends the sky
And the Lord of hosts descends upon the earth,
To wipe away the tears of those who cry
And replace them with the tears of joy and mirth.

For a young boy on the farm being cooped up in the house all winter, nothing was looked forward to more than the end of the cold weather and the beginning of spring. Shoes would come off, and one could play barefoot outside, with such wonderful games as tag, hide and seek, dare base, kick ball, and kick the can. This particular poem was an attempt on my part to write in the Emily Dickinson style.

Old Man Winter

The snow is melting on the hills,
The Ice is full of doubt;
The winds are blowing softer now
And less inclined to pout.

A pride of daffodils arise
To strut their frocks of green;
The birds are flying from the south
And singing for the queen.

The cows are lowing in the stalls,
The horses kick the air;
Old man winter's weak and wane,
And rocking in his chair.

MOSES L. HOCHSTETLER

What we learn in our childhood goes a long way in shaping who we are as adults. This poem expresses some of the warm memories that still shape my attitudes and outlook in life.

I Dream Of Yesterday

I dream of yesterday,
A simple time, carefree;
With Mamma fixing supper,
Brother playing games,
Sister at the table
And I'm on Daddy's knee.

I dream of days gone by
When I was still quite small,
I was tucked into bed:
Cozy, warm, and snug;
And I slept all night long
Until the breakfast call.

I dream of olden times
When Daddy stoked the coals;
Brother brought the hickory in
And made the fire roar,
Mamma poured the cider
And passed the home made rolls.

I dream of yesterday
When cares were sparse and few.
Daddy did the chores at night
And plowed the fields by day;
Sister read me story books:
Some fairy tales, some true.

I dream of days gone by
When family meant a lot.
We had no television
Back home on the farm,
But Daddy always said
"Be thankful what you've got!"

I dream of long ago
When horses pulled the sleighs,
We did not rush here and there,
Cars were seldom seen,
Neighbors helped out neighbors
In many different ways.

I dream of yesterday,
A simple time carefree.
But I plan for tomorrow,
Glad to be alive;
Having learned from yesterday
To live and love to be.

When we are children, we can hardly wait to grow into adulthood. Once we become adults with adult responsibilities, we miss the comforts and privileges we enjoyed as children. One thing is certain: our "Fleeting Youth" is gone before we know it.

Fleeting Youth

How fleeting youth!
It is even as the tide
When it rises before the storm.
It neither hesitates nor procrastinates:
It rushes in with all its might,
It swells in pride and power,
It thunders in its magnificence,
It roars in its majesty,
It assails every obstacle,
It tackles every rock and reef,
It plunders the shoals,
It pounds the granite boulder
Etching into the status quo,
It smashes barriers;
Forever leaving its mark.
It screams its defiance,
It flows, it ebbs,
And then it is gone.

This poem reflects the memories of when the whole family was all still at home under one roof. My oldest brother is 18 years older than I am, and he was married and moved out of the house when I was five years old, so I didn't experience the whole family together for very long.

I Dreamed of Home Again last Night

I dreamed of home again last night,
Of Elmer and brothers Ed,
Of Mary as she lit the lamp,
Of Millie's home-made bread;
I saw Father stoke the coals,
And Mother's beaming face;
I dreamed that I was there last night;
Back in the old home place.

I dreamed that I saw Junior there,
And Mel with Lydia Mae,
With John and Jonas hard at work
To hunt the day away;
LaMar was doing chores again,
With Esther helping out;
And Ray and Rudy on their bikes
Were riding all about.

A dream refreshes memories,
And brings back days of yore,
Though what we had those youthful days
Will be again no more.
For life is but a fleeting thing:
A flash, a fading star—
But memories continue on
And make us who we are.

Back home on the farm, I would often waken to the sound of roosters crowing, birds singing, and the sun streaming in through the southeastern window of my upstairs bedroom. I could look out my window to the east and see our lovely grape arbor below; apple, pear, apricot, cherry, and plum trees farther east, and beyond that the waving fields of grain with woodlands and trees in the misty horizon.

Sparkling Good Morning

It's a sparkling good morning,
It's a brand spanking new day;
The glistening dew is adorning
The crimson crowned buds of hay.

The crisp misty morning air
As fresh as a cold spring stream;
Greets me as I rise to share
A moment in life's conscious dream.

The wind whispers softly through,
Gently kissing the green leaves;
A fleecy cloud in golden hue
Drifts buoyantly above my eaves.

Birds are singing, O, what cheer!
Joyful sounds that fill the air;
Jubilation far and near,
Such a morning bright and fair!

Once in a while I force myself to write a free (non-rhyming) verse, and this particular one covers some of the same memories as those expressed in "Whispers of the U-Creek."

Kindred Memories

The fleecy clouds are laced
with silver ribbons,
the south wind blows softly
'cross the meadow,
bringing me the scent of
new-mown hay.
Down beyond the cottonwoods
the U-creek meanders,
with the pungent smell
of water, weeds and fish . . .
crayfish dart by swiftly
in the current.
Minnows swim in sheer delight,
frogs splash in deftly
from the banks;
how sweet the day does
rouse the kindred memories
of a barefoot boy
the decades left behind . . .
running through the clover
in the summertime,
wallowing the creek
up to his thighs,
and laughing at
the richness of it all.

The Amish in the community where I was raised had some strange customs and traditions surrounding January 6th (Epiphany or "Old Christmas" as they call it). This date was much more frightening to me as a child than Halloween ever was. Some of the tales listed in this poem, among others, kept being repeated among the Amish children of our community, causing a great deal of consternation and apprehension.

January Sixth

According to tradition,
Strange things happen
On January the sixth,
Between the witching hours
Of eleven-twelve PM;
Don't go into the barn
Because the animals
Will talk to you,
And perhaps even tell you
Of the day when you will die.

And never ever place a mirror
Underneath your pillow
During this frightful night . . .
If you do you may see
The one that you will marry,
Or perhaps the Devil himself
Will reflect back at you
With an awful wicked grin
To give you such a scare
That you may wish you were dead.

Once when I was just a lad
A neighbor boy laughed
At all these traditions,
And placed a mirror
Beneath his sleep-pillow
On just such a night,
And awoke to hear a chain
Clinking up the stairs—
So he broke the mirror
And all went deathly quiet.

Another older man in our
Neighborhood of Amish
Went out into the barn
And the horses spoke to him
Of horrible things
He never dared repeat,
So be careful what you do
On January the sixth.
Do not tempt fate . . .
Or take the Devil lightly.

If you have never witnessed a brilliant rainbow in the country, you have missed one of the greatest wonders of this world. Sometimes it seems that you are able to see the very spot the rainbow touches the ground, on both ends of the bow, but don't ever try to find the pot of gold at the end of the rainbow, because as you get closer to where the bow touches down, it keeps moving to some other area!

Rainbow

A flash of brilliant summer-green,
A kiss of heaven-blue,
The red, orange, and yellow sheen
Of sun on morning dew.

The lavender the lilacs love,
In spring when flowers bloom;
The rainbow weaves the colors of
This world on her loom.

The sonnet below reflects my memories of when I, as a teenager, delighted in sitting in the shade of a cottonwood, a walnut, a wild cherry, or an aspen tree, as I rested the horses before plowing another furrow around a field. It gave me time for contemplation as I watched the clouds, or listened to the birds chirp and sing.

Sonnet of Peace

At even tide, when all is calm at last,
And I sit quiet 'neath the aspen shade,
With summer's sky in golden amber cast
Above my blissful verdant grassy glade:
Where wind-caressed red clover buds do spill
Their sweetly distilled perfume everywhere,
While cheerful leaves about me hum and trill,
And songs of birds festoon the magic air
With melodies so lovely heaven-sent
I seldom think a worried thought, or bring
To mind a dark and dreary sad moment,
And then it is my heart does gladly sing
And dance within my awed and humble breast;
To contemplate of life so richly blest.

Scarecrows were quite common in the neighborhood where I grew up. My older brothers made one and placed it in our garden to keep, not just crows, but hopefully many other birds at bay.

Scarecrow

He wears a stocking cap of red,
And gloves of white and blue;
His hair is yellow straw of wheat
Still damp with morning dew.

His eyes are bleak and rather drawn,
His beard a shuck of corn;
And still he wears the overalls
He wore when he was borne.

He stands out near the garden fence
All sober and astute;
He does his job around the clock
Though blind, and deaf, and mute.

For most of my childhood we did not have running water in our home: cold or hot. Thus, the "Outhouse out back" was our only "rest room." We had no cause for complaint, but imagine, if you will, sitting on a ring of ice every time you used the toilet—which is what the toilet seats of the outhouse felt like in the winter months. On blustery and windy snow days, it was not uncommon to have to brush the snow off the seat first!

The Outhouse Out Back

Some say that the old days
Were quaint and held charm,
But what I remember
Back home on the farm,
Are cold winter mornings
And cold winter nights,
Working hard the day long,
And late with dim lights,
And when I had to go
I faced the cold fact;
I had no place to go
But the outhouse out back!

Work, it seemed, on our 120 acre dairy farm was never done. There were always jobs to do, and sometimes there were 3 or 4 things that needed done at the same time. A rainy day was always welcome, as it afforded us a kind of vacation day.

Our Work Is Not Done Yet

The cows are awaiting their milking,
The horses need fed in the stall,
The eggs have yet to be gathered,
Our work is not done yet, at all.

The windmill's in need of a greasing,
The harnesses need a repair;
We must grind the corn for the cattle,
And clean out the pen for the mare.

The wheat is in need of replanting,
But first we must ready the ground;
The fence needs fixed where it's broken—
There's lots of such work still around.

The wood in the bin is diminished,
It has to be filled in the fall.
Winter, it seems, is approaching;
Our work is not done yet, at all.

"Shorty" was a smaller "gelding" horse with a big heart who would literally have worked until he dropped if we would have allowed it. One advantage of using horses to work the fields over tractors is that a man can develop affection for a horse in a way that isn't possible with a tractor. But then, when a tractor "dies" it doesn't seem quite so tragic.

Shorty, a Horse of a Different Color

It's been near fifty years ago,
But I remember it like yesterday . . .
When a weak and spindly colt was born
In a cold and snowy spring;
Such gangly legs, and a small star
Plastered off-center on his too-big head,
"Not much good for nuthin" Dad said,
But he proved us all wrong
With a heart the size of Gibraltar
And a spirit of the restless west wind
Driving his legs and rippling shoulders;
Fully grown he could thunder
Across the pastures far ahead
Of the other "good" draft horses,
And hitched to the sod-plow
Shorty would pull twice his share,
And by nightfall when the
Other bigger ones were lagging
And their single-trees were sagging
He would pull the plow alone,
And would have died rather than quit;
That's the kind of horse he was,
And in the early fall of sixty-three
He lit out of the barn in full stride
And ran into the end of a steel gate,
And Shorty came to his sudden end,
And I mourned for him as a man
Would mourn for his friend.

Who hasn't had a relative or friend of the family that prepared food that we would rather not have had to eat? The name of this relative has been changed to protect the guilty!

Aunt Matildy's Soup

We would gather 'round the table
At my aunt Matildy's place,
And she'd spread her bestest dishes out
And napkins trimmed with lace;
Then she'd take the biggest kettle
Off the stove a-boilin' hot,
And she'd fill our bowls to brim full
With that stuff from that old pot.
I would reckon sure as shootin'
It was like the time before,
When she served that same concoction
And I spilt it on the floor;
For it tasted so disgustin'
That I claimed I'd never stoop,
So low that I would eat again
My Aunt Matildy's soup.

Now I know that Aunt Matildy
Must have done the best she could,
And my mamma complimented her
And said "How awf'ly good!"
And my dad was quick to state that
"It's quite an undertakin',"
But when they got away from her
They'd start to belly achin'.

"And why?" my dad would always say,
A loos'nin' up his belt,
"Why do I always leave her place
The worst I ever felt?"
He didn't have to answer that,
I knew it was that scoop
That held too much, yes, way too much,
Of Aunt Matildy's soup

She must have added noodles
Made of eggs a mite too old,
And dried out bits of carrots that
Were crusted green with mold,
And I suppose she scraped the table
For a week or two, at least,
For scraps of beef 'n' chicken bones
Not fit for man or beast.
Now the smell of it was strangely
Like the smell of spoilt meat—
So I ask you, no, I beg you,
Not to make me sit and eat
That gristly mix that gags you
And will knock you for a loop;
Not a solitary spoon full of
My Aunt Matildy's soup.

The inspiration for this particular poem was my Aunt; a twin sister to my mother, who stayed with us in our home a good part of my childhood years. She was the hardest working woman I have ever had the pleasure of knowing, and she did these, as well as many other things not listed here!

When Rosie O'Riley Cleans the House

When Rosie O'Riley cleans the house
It's quite a sight to see;
When Rosie O'Riley cleans the house
It's clean as clean can be.
She fluffs the pillows, makes the beds,
And wipes the dirty walls;
She sweeps and mops and cleans the floors
And shines the dingy halls.
She dusts the furniture with ease
And makes the woodwork glow;
When Rosie O'Riley cleans the house
It's really quite a show.
She rushes here, she rushes there,
And quickly does her work;
She whistles tunes, she sings and croons,
And makes the coffee perk;
And when she takes a morning break
To fix the breakfast meal,
She sighs and flicks her hair aside,
And says "It's no big deal."

When Rosie O'Riley cleans the house
It's clean throughout the week;
You'll never see a grungy drape,
Nor see a grimy streak.
She cleans the windows, spiffs the glass,
And makes the mirrors new,
She washes, dries, and folds the clothes,
And does the dishes, too.
She mows the lawn and rakes the leaves

And bags them all away;
She trims the hedges nice and neat,
And never asks for pay.
She rushes here, she rushes there,
And makes her mother proud,
She whistles tunes, she sings and croons
And ne'er complains aloud;
Just smiles and flicks her hair aside
And says "It's no big deal,
Some days I do a whole lot more,
It's all in how I feel."

When Rosie O'Riley cleans the house
Her work has just begun.
She plows the fields and plants the corn,
And still her work's not done.
She cleans the stables, milks the cows,
And beds them down at night;
She strains the milk, and takes the cream,
And churns it thick and white.
She heaps it on the pies she bakes
And serves them to her guests;
Then gets their coats and sees them off
Before she goes and rests.
She rushes here, she rushes there,
And seldom gets much sleep.
She whistles tunes, she sings and croons,
And earns her board and keep.
She smiles and flicks her hair aside,
And says "It's no big deal."
Some day someone will marry her
For more than sex appeal!

This is a true account of a vivid dream I had as a youngster. All I knew of poetry at the time was Mother Goose and Nursery rhymes, and my brothers and sisters reciting James Whitcomb Riley's "Little Orphant Annie."

Wonder In Their Eyes

When I was just a young lad
And barely into school,
Just learning to speak English;
For at home we spoke what some
Would call a lower German,
I was so painfully shy,
And stumbled over my words,
So embarrassed to answer
Even when asked a simple thing
Like "What is your name?"
Or "How old are you, son?"

'Twas then I had a wondrous dream
That I was out in the barn,
Standing atop a granary bin,
And down below me, gathered there,
A huge expectant crowd,
All looking up at me
With wonder in their eyes,
As from my mouth there came
A stream of poetry so delightful
With effortless ease and joy,
As to amaze myself and them.

But it wasn't until much later
After I had lived two-score,
That I found that somewhere deep
Inside there was indeed a fount
Of words and phrases, rhymes,
And reasons, just waiting to
Flow out, and to be shared with
That huge expectant crowd;
And though I'm not there
Inside that barn looking down,
I do see the people of my dream . . .

    With wonder in their eyes.

Whether it is global warming, a slight change in the climate, or something else entirely, today there are many more geese that spend the winter in northern Indiana than when I was a youth. At that time, all geese except for the domesticated ones, flew south for the winter. When they were seen heading south, one could be certain cold weather was right around the corner.

When the Geese Fly By

Coming from the cold north,
Forming a vee,
Beating their wings
Austerely:
South to a pleasant
And balmier clime;
Sounding their requiem.

The dandelions'
And the thistles' down;
Long ago buried
In the fallow ground.
The last of the mournful
Autumn winds sigh,
When the geese fly by.

Drumming to the heart's beat,
Drumming "defeat",
Sounding taps for
The fall's retreat.
Ashes in the fireplace
Flicker to a flame,
Sparked by the passing game.

The sky turns gray
And the grasses fade,
The frost stays white
In the morning shade.
The last leaves of summer
Turn brown and die,
When the geese fly by.

I include this poem because my parent's home, food, and beds were always there for friends, relatives, and even passers-by who needed a place to spend the night. Many a night the youngest children slept on blankets on the floor in order to make the beds available for guests. This poem reflects a philosophy my parents imparted to me.

Welcome!

This home shall be a haven
In a world full of care;
We do not have a lot, my friend,
But what we have we share.

Come join us at the table,
There's food and drink in store;
Partake of what we have, my friend,
For that's what friends are for.

Relax and take your shoes off,
We do not mind at all;
And if you need to rest, my friend,
The bedroom's down the hall.

We may not be aristocrats,
Nor yet be nobles, but
You're always welcome here, my friend,
Within our humble hut.

This home shall be a haven
In a world full of care;
We do not have a lot, my friend,
But what we have we share.

My parents had 17 children in 18 years. Three of my older brothers I never met. The twins Ervin and Mervin died shortly after birth, and Gilbert died when about one month old. Our house was somewhat crowded with all 14 of us siblings under one roof. One has to wonder what it would have been like with three more in the house. It certainly would have changed everything.

Shadows of the Grave

Ervin, Mervin, and Gilbert;
Three brothers of mine
Whom I have never known,
And never in this life will get to know.
Ervin and Mervin died at birth;
Gilbert lived a little while,
But long before I came along
They came and went.

Ervin, Mervin, and Gilbert,
Three brothers of mine;
Graves marked with simple stones
In a cemetery, while I linger
Many days and months; many years
On beyond their time.
I would not be the same today
Had they lived on.

Ervin, Mervin, and Gilbert,
Three brothers of mine
Whom I have never known;
But still and all they leave a vacancy;
Brothers of the womb—now merely
Shadows of the grave.
I shall not see them in this life—
But some day soon.

This particular poem describes a view I had looking out the west window of the first bedroom I slept in after moving upstairs. The bedroom was above our kitchen, and I shared it with 3 older brothers. During the winter month, the room got cold enough to freeze water if left in a glass, and when we got up in the morning, we would grab our pants and pull them up on the way down stairs, so we wouldn't have to stand on the ice-cold floor any longer than necessary.

A View From My Window

I could see the evergreens swaying in the breeze:
The maples tall and handsome,
The lilac's blushing cheek;
I could see the fields of grain waving in the wind,
And in the distance; willow rows
Along the Helmuth Creek.

I could see the dusky woods along the county road;
A sky that's turned to amber
As evenings unfold;
I could see the sparkling stars sprinkled in the sky,
And see the moonlight blanketing
The world in burnished gold.

Wide open spaces and the beauty of nature combine to make farm life a most pleasant and interesting experience for a youngster. The saying that "you can take the boy out of the country, but you can't take the country out of the boy" was certainly true in my case. I am still a country boy at heart.

Beauty Around Us

Lyric to the old Irish melody of "Galway Bay"

There's the smell of budding clover in the meadows,
There's the scent of violets blooming in the glen;
In the valley daisies peek out from the shadows
Of the willows as if chicks beneath the hen.

See the beauty of the lilies in the morning,
See the grace that they display for everyone;
See the colors of the rose adorn the evening,
As you watch the glory of the setting sun.

O the wonder of the ravens and the eagles,
Of the swallows as they glide upon the air;
Hear the singing of the birds out in the pine trees
And the whistling of the whippoorwill so fair.

See the butterflies go gliding on the breezes,
See the summer clouds billow in the sky;
See the leaves in autumn turn to gold and amber
And the yellow daffodils when spring comes by.

There's the beauty of stars up in the heavens,
There's the beauty of the land and of the sea;
Yes, there's beauty in the universe around us
That the Lord our God has made for you and me.

The lovely pink and white peonies that bloomed in our front yard and the wonderfully scented lilacs that grew close to our house were Mother's favorite flowers. To this day, I cannot pass them by without thinking of her.

The Lilacs Are Blooming

(Song Lyrics)

The lilacs are blooming, are blooming dear sister,
The lilacs are blooming this spring;
The robin is building her nest in the arbor,
The bluebirds and gold finches sing.
We'll walk through the meadow together, dear sister,
We'll walk through the meadow today,
We'll skip through the clover, the daisies, the violets,
And breathe in the mint on our way.

    Refrain:

    Our mother, dear mother, did so love the lilacs,
    And waited for them to appear;
    She watched for the robins and listened for song birds
    To sing their sweet songs in her ear.

The chorus of song birds would make Mother cheerful,
The lilacs would give her a smile,
Sweet clover; bright daisies and violets, dear sister,
Would ease all her burdens awhile.
Our mother would gather the mint from the meadow
To make us a sweet pot of tea,
She'd steep it, she'd pour it, she'd serve it, dear sister:
For family; for you, and for me.

    Refrain:

Rivel soup is a common Amish soup made by dropping little "rivels" (chunks) of flour and eggs into hot milk. Bruckel soup is a cold summer-time soup made by combining pieces of bread, fruit, sugar, and milk. Baby soup is made by adding pieces of bread to hot milk, and adding some butter, salt and pepper. Tomato gravy is made by thickening tomato juice with flour and adding a little milk or cream. These, along with corn pone, chicken noodles, rice, and beans, were among the staples of our diet.

Corn Pone and Rivel Soup

(Song Lyrics)

Pennyroyal in the morning, Oh! It smelled so good!
I'd have a cup again right now, if I only could!
How I liked tomato gravy covering my plate;
Couldn't see my eggs and bread; that is how we ate!

Corn pone and rivel soup, liverwurst and mush;
Bruckle soup and baby soup, there's no need to rush.

Brother's in the field a-plowing, ring that dinner bell!
Sister got the table ready, and she did it well!
There's a feast of chicken noodles, beans, and boiled rice;
For dessert there's apple dumplings, and it's mighty nice!

Corn pone and rivel soup, liverwurst and mush;
Bruckle soup and baby soup, there's no need to rush.

Dad is milking cows tonight, won't be in till late;
Supper's ready on the table, I can hardly wait!
Mother made us all a meal out of milk and bread,
She made sure we had enough to keep us fully fed!

Corn pone and rivel soup, liverwurst and mush;
Bruckle soup and baby soup, there's no need to rush.

ESSAYS

Maple Syrup Season

As a child, I always looked forward to Maple syrup season. It was one of the earliest big undertakings of the year. A lot of preparation had to go into it. Dad had to set up the big evaporator pan on our giant furnace out in the wash house. Many Amish have "sugar camps" out in the woods, so they don't have to haul the maple sap as far. We had a big furnace in our wash house that served a number of different purposes. It was used to heat water for the washing machine (no hot water heaters for us at that time). The same furnace was used to make apple butter in the fall, and to boil down hog fat in the winter to make lard.

After the pan was set up and checked to make sure there were no leaks, hundreds of galvanized buckets had to be thoroughly washed and cleaned, along with the spigots to insert in the maple trees. Then, Dad would make sure we had plenty of firewood on hand, because once the sap boiling begins, there is very little time to go get more wood. When Dad was convinced that the weather was turning warmer (about late February or early March) he and the boys would take a wagon load of buckets back to the woods, and tap the trees. Each maple of about 14 inches in diameter, or bigger, had to have a small hole drilled by hand, a spigot inserted, and a bucket hung on the spigot. Some of the bigger maples got two buckets. The buckets held about three gallons each.

The fun really began when we got a good thaw. In order to get a good run of sap from the maple trees, we needed a strong freeze at night, and a good thaw during the day. The more freezes and thaws you get, the more maple sap one can draw from the trees. Each time we'd get a good thaw, we'd have to hitch the team of horses to the "mud boat" that had a 150 gallon tank on it, and we'd go out to gather the sap. The mud boat was really more of a sleigh, with wide runners that would glide easily across wet ground and through mud. It was hard work to gather the sap. The bigger boys and adults would take two five-gallon buckets, one in each hand. The smaller boys and women usually struggled with one five-gallon, or carried two smaller buckets. I remember what an accomplishment it was when I was finally big and strong enough to carry a five-gallon bucket in each hand. Sometimes the buckets on the trees were only half full, and you could go through the woods rather quickly. At other times, the buckets were almost all running over, and it took a lot of time and effort to gather it all, carry it to the bigger tank, and dump it in. The horses knew the route, and followed the trail through the woods without having to be driven. All we had to do was yell "giddy-up" and "whoa."

It wasn't unusual to have two and three tanks full of sap to drive up to the furnace in one day. The woods were the better part of a half mile from our wash house. In the one side of our wash house was a bigger 500 gallon tank. When there were several days of freezes and thaws in a row, this tank would be brim full, and the smaller tank would be waiting for room to empty it. In such cases, Dad would boil sap all night, taking off as many as two and three batches of syrup. Usually there were between 8 and 12 gallons taken off at a time. The smell of sap evaporating is one of the sweetest smells in the world, and we enjoyed pure maple syrup on our pancakes all year.

    I don't know about many of the other Amish in our community, but my dad had a tradition of taking the last, leftover, half-sap, half-syrup, (you could never cook it all down into syrup, because you had to have a continual supply of sap to push the partially boiled sap down to the far end of the pan) put it in a big wooden barrel, added yeast, and let it ferment into what we called "sugar water beer." This was a most wonderful treat, even for us youngsters, as the alcohol content was so miniscule that one couldn't get "tipsy" over it. It had a taste unlike anything else in this world, and made the most delicious drink that we enjoyed for a number of weeks (first it had to ferment for a few weeks) after the maple syrup season was over and done with.

Shocking Wheat and Oats

When the wheat was ripe enough to cut, Dad would get the binder out of storage the day before the job was to commence, and make sure everything was in working order. All moving parts had to be lubricated, the chains and the canvas conveyer belt had to be working properly, and the cutting sickle sharp. The twine had to be properly threaded through the machinery, to make sure the bundles would get properly bound and tied. This was no job for a novice. Dad was a good mechanic, and had a keen general knowledge of how things worked. The binder, in our estimation, was a complicated piece of machinery and a technological wonder. Never mind that many of our neighbors were using automated combines. A large wheel with steel treads was located under the binder that powered the cutting sickles, the conveyer belt, and the binding machinery. There was no gasoline or diesel engine involved.

As soon as the milking and the other morning chores were done in the barn, Dad would harness three horses and hitch them to the binder. In short order he would be "opening up the field" by cutting a swath of wheat off around the outer edge of the field, moving counter-clockwise, so the sickles would cut the wheat closest to the fence. The binder would kick out sheaves of wheat, neatly tied in bundles, or "sheaves". All us boys would follow around behind the binder on the first "go-round" to move the sheaves out of the way, because on the next "go-round" the horses had to walk where the sheaves were pitched by the binder. On all future trips, the binder would go clockwise around the field, so the horses wouldn't be trampling down the standing uncut wheat. By the time Dad had gone around the field twice, it was time for the boys to start shocking the wheat. The first two sheaves were set up leaning against each other, one to the north, and one to the south. Two more sheaves were set up the same way, on the west side of the first two, leaning against each other, and leaning slightly against the first pair of sheaves. Another pair was set up on the east side of the others, also leaning slightly toward the center pair. Sometimes, if the wheat was not too moist, another bundle was added in the center of the north and south sides. Finally, the last bundle was taken and carefully fanned out to spread over the top of all the standing bundles, with the grain heads pointing mostly toward the west and down over the shock. This served several purposes. It helped to bind all the sheaves together and solidify the shock, and it served as a canopy over the entire shock, causing the rain to run off, rather than into, the shock. Attention was paid to directions, because most of the strong winds would come out of the west or northwest. Usually it took 3 to 4 good "shockers" to shock an entire 10 acres in one day. An accomplished shocker could set up shocks that would withstand rather strong and stiff windstorms. Occasionally, storms would get strong enough to blow down a number of shocks, whereupon we were obliged to go back into the field and set them up again.

Shocking wheat is an arduous task, especially if the temperature is into the upper eighties or into the nineties. This was one reason Dad always wanted to get into the field while it was still cool in the morning. As the day heated up, the horses had to rest more often so they would not to get overheated and exhausted. Those of us who shocked the wheat would usually wear long-sleeved shirts. Wheat straw can be very sharp and harsh. Shocking wheat for very long can leave bare arms scratched and bleeding in a hurry. With our long-sleeved shirts, sweat would soon pour down our foreheads and into our eyes. Sometimes, if it would get too unbearably hot, we would "give it up" and go back out later in the cool of the evening. Many times we would be shocking after sundown in the moonlight. If we couldn't finish that evening or night, we would have to get out early the next day and finish the job.

Oats were generally a little easier to shock, as the straw was not as sharp and harsh and more pliable. Unlike harvesting with combines when the grain is good and dry, cutting with a binder had to be done before the wheat and oats were totally dry, or too much grain would be lost. The shocks were set up and allowed to dry several more weeks before they could be threshed.

Threshing Day

To a young Amish child, threshing day can be the most exciting day of the year. Between the ages of 3 and 6, my brother and I would stand by the kitchen window of our home, peering down the gravel road to our north, watching for the first sign of the big Rumbly oil-pull tractor pulling the threshing rig to our farm. Preparation for this day started several days before the big event. The straw shed part of our barn had to be cleared of all debris that had accumulated there the past several months: odd and end pieces of lumber, tools, toys, and even bales of straw had to be cleared out (we always ran out of straw about 4 or 5 month before threshing, so Dad had to buy baled straw to use until threshing time). The granary bin had to be thoroughly cleaned. The women had pies and cakes to bake, chickens to dress; salads, noodles, dressings, and Jello to prepare; to feed the hungry crew lunch the next day. The house had to be cleaned and the yard made presentable.

A big wash tub (the kind used by those who owned the old ringer laundry washers) had to be set up in the front yard. Early in the morning, before the threshing crew arrived, the tub was filled with cold water. That way, by the time the threshing crew came in to eat at noon, the water would be tepid, and they could wash themselves comfortably; a formidable job, because the threshing crew would generally be covered with chaff and dirt. An hour or two before the actual threshing rig arrived, empty wagons pulled by teams of horses started coming into our driveway, usually followed by a man on a bicycle or in a buggy. It took a wagon handler, and a "pitcher" to load each wagon; both carried a three pronged pitchfork. They would head immediately for the field of shocked wheat or oats, and start loading. The "pitcher" stayed on the ground, and "pitched" the sheaves up to the wagon handler, who would carefully place the sheaves on the wagon. It takes experience and know-how to properly stack the sheaves evenly and have them be properly balanced on the wagon. The sheaves had to be stacked in such a way so that they wouldn't bounce or slide off at every little dip and bump the wagon wheels hit in the field.

About eight O'clock in the morning, if our farm was the first to be threshed that day, my brother and I could expect to see the slow moving threshing rig coming down the road toward us. Every once in awhile, the Rumbly tractor would send a big cloud of black diesel smoke billowing skyward. As it came closer to our drive we could hear the "chew, chew, chew" noise of the Rumbly, and we watched in awe as the whole rig stopped right in front of our house to unhitch the caboose. The caboose was where the extra diesel fuel, belts, spare parts, grease, oil, and tools were stored. Finally the threshing machine was pulled into the barn yard, and backed up to the barn. The blower was raised up to a small sliding door on the side of the straw shed. The tractor was then pulled about 30 to 35 feet away, facing the threshing machine. A large heavy flat belt, probably eight to ten inches wide, was looped over the main threshing machine drive wheel, and looped over the belt drive wheel on the Rumbly. Everything had to be perfectly lined up, and the tension on the belt just right. In order to run the threshing machine properly, there always had to be a half twist in the belt at the middle, so that the belt on top of the drive wheel on the tractor would meet the bottom of the drive wheel at the threshing rig.

By the time the threshing machine was set and ready to go, the first wagon loads of sheaves were waiting to start feeding the hungry beast. Two wagons would pull up to the machine, one on each side. As the Rumbly revved the thresher up to full speed, belts and chains would begin to move, wheels and pulleys begin to whir, and the wagon handlers quickly started pitching the sheaves onto the front conveyer belt, where they would be drawn into the mouth of the machine, chewed up, and gulped down into the belly of the monstrosity. One could hear the work load increase on the Rumbly as more black smoke billowed out. You could literally feel the ground shake. In short order straw would begin belching out of the blower, and the grain would start to pour out of the auger into a waiting wagon. To a child, nothing could have been more exciting.

Putting Hay Away

When I was a youngster, my father put hay in our barn loose. Most Amish now have their hay baled. I was probably around 10 years old when we finally started baling ours, but it was putting the loose hay in the barn that involved the greatest amount of work, and was the most exciting for us youngsters. I remember going with Dad to town to buy the rope to replace the older rope that was getting too worn. It took one inch rope to bear the bundle of loose hay that had to be drawn up to the very gable of the barn. From there, three-quarter inch rope was sufficient to pull the bundle along the gable track to either of the three hay mows in our barn. Everything was ingeniously rigged on pulleys, and a kind of block and tackle attached to a dolly on the track, and set up so that it would self lock when the bundle of hay was drawn up to the gable.

There were basically two types of hay that Dad raised for the farm: timothy to feed the horses, and either alfalfa, clover, or a mixture of the two for the cattle. Hay was cut with a horse-drawn "hay mower." The cutting sickle was powered with the mower's ridged wheels. After the hay was cut and dried for several days, a special horse drawn "rake" would rake the hay into windrows. Usually, in good drying weather, by the end of the third day after it was cut, the hay was ready to be put into the barn.

A special "hay loader" was hooked to the back of the wagon. A rope "sling" with wooden cross bars was laid out on the floor of the wagon, being careful to leave the ends tied up on the front and rear uprights where they could be found later. The slings came in two sections; held together in the center by a special trip mechanism. As the team of horses straddled the windrows, the hay would be "raked" up the loader and dumped into the wagon. One or two of my brothers would carefully spread the hay out over the sling. By the time I was 6 years old, I was guiding the team over the windrows to load the wagon. The horses followed the windrows, but when the row turned at the corner, the horses had to walk on past and make a slow turn, or the corner would be missed. Care had to be taken not to turn too sharply, or the whole wagon could be capsized. When the hay was about 4 or 5 feet deep on the wagon, another sling was laid out on top of the already loaded hay. Hay was then loaded until the wagon was full and well rounded at the top. The heavy top sling load would always compress the bottom load to about 3 feet instead of the 4 or 5 feet when loaded. Once the wagon was full, the loader was unhitched, and the wagon pulled up to the barn. A team of horses had their work cut out in pulling a loaded hay wagon up the "bank" leading to the hay mow section of the barn. Many bank barns are still around; a leftover reminder of the time when all farmers put their hay in the barn loose. Once the loaded wagon was inside the barn, the heavy load bearing rope was attached to the first sling load. Another team of horses was waiting on the outside of the barn, hitched to the end of the main weight-bearing rope. The first sling load was then pulled about five feet off of the wagon, and a trip rope attached to the bottom center of the sling, onto the trip mechanism. The huge bundle was then pulled the rest of the way up to the very top of the barn gable, and locked into place; the whole load swaying precariously back and forth.

Once hoisted to the top, the outside team of horses had to be hitched to the side pulling rope, and the load was pulled to whichever hay mow that Dad wanted the hay in. When in place, someone had to take the long trip road, stand well back out of the way, and "trip" the sling, so the bottom would separate, and the hay would fall down. The first few tripped loads would always come down with a thunderous noise and a burst of wind; dust and chaff flying everywhere. As the hay got deeper in the mow, the load had less distance to fall, and a "softer" place to land. The next sling load was immediately pulled up, over, and tripped. Someone then had the arduous task of leveling the hay in the mow, while others would go out and load the wagon once again. With temperatures reaching the nineties in July, and no breeze in the barn, the leveler would get drenched in sweat, not to mention getting covered with chaff and dust

Making Apple Butter

Making apple butter was the highlight of the fall season. It was an all day affair, and made further use of the big brick furnace in the wash-house. As with many other major jobs on an Amish farm, preparation for making apple butter began days before the event. The Hochstetler farm had five or six good sized apple trees, three large pear trees, plums, apricots, and sweet and sour cherry trees to the east of the house, in what we termed the "baum garta" (tree garden). We had another much larger orchard to the south of the house, east of the truck patch, where Dad had a number of Red, Yellow, and Golden Delicious, Grimes Golden, Winesap, Jonathan, and Macintosh apple trees, along with peach trees, blackberry, and raspberry brambles. When enough of the apples were getting ripe, the family pitched in to pick numerous crates and bushels of apples for cider and for "schnitz" apples. The day before the apple butter was to be made, a wagon was loaded with crates of apples to take to the cider mill, about 10 miles south of where we lived. Pulled by heavy draft horses, it was an all day job getting there, grinding the apples, pressing the cider out of the pulp, and returning home.

The same day my brothers would take the apples to make cider, Dad would remove the big cast-iron wash-water kettle from the furnace, and replace it with the big copper kettle. I would guess it held somewhere between 30 and 40 gallons of liquid. The big kettle had to be thoroughly scrubbed, washed, and cleaned for the next day. Even though it was always stored upside down so it wouldn't get dusty inside, after sitting empty all year, it needed a thorough cleaning and sterilizing. Dad would also make sure there was enough fire wood on hand to complete the job the next day. In the house, Mom and my sisters would be busy peeling, coring, and slicing apples for the big event.

Early the following morning, Dad and my brothers would fill the big kettle with cider, and Dad would start the fire in the furnace. In less than an hour, the steam started rolling out of the big kettle. We had a large wooden stir apparatus that had about a nine or ten foot handle on it, so we could stand well back from the heat. At the end of the handle, the stir part went straight down at a right angle, and was about two and a half feet long and six inches wide, with big round holes in it. The cider had to be constantly stirred, to prevent burning on the bottom of the kettle. I was obligated to take my turn at stirring at a very early age. Also, as the apple butter neared completion, it was necessary to have a long handle on the stirring stick, because the thick boiling mixture would splatter considerably as the bubbles burst on the surface.

As some of the cider steamed away, more would be added. By mid-afternoon it was time to add the apple "schnitz" (slices of pealed apples). Quite often Mom would also add apple sauce she had made for that purpose, and sometimes sliced pears would be put into the mixture. When the schnitz had all dissolved in the boiling mixture, it was time to add the cinnamon and the sugar. This was all boiled together until it was determined that the cider would no longer separate from the apple pulp. The fire was then allowed to die down, and a block and tackle, attached to a small dolly and track on the wash-house rafters, was then used to lift the kettle off the furnace, and lower it to the floor. Mom had prepared about twelve or fifteen crocks, each big enough to hold a gallon, and the hot apple butter was dipped to within about 2 inches of the top of the crocks. Mother would then put a newspaper over the top of the crock, several pages thick, and tie a string around the paper to hold it in place. The apple butter would form its own thick gel at the top as it cooled, which served as a "seal" that would keep the apple butter from spoiling all year long.

This may sound like a lot of apple butter, and it was, but apple butter was the main bread spread of our household, and with sixteen living under one roof, many of them growing boys, you can begin to see that it would take a lot of spread. Our apple butter was nothing like the grocery store variety, but was thicker, much darker, and much more flavorful. Commercially prepared apple butter has nowhere near the concentrated cider content that ours had. Most of the commercial varieties seem to be dehydrated apple sauce with cinnamon and other spices added. Comparing theirs with what we had is like comparing apples and oranges.

Butchering Day

Long before butchering day, Dad would select a young cow, heifer, or ox to be butchered. The animal would then be fed extra grain to add weight. Butchering day was always in the winter. Dad tried to pick a day that was cold enough to freeze the ground, but not cold enough to freeze the meat. If it's too cold, hands get too cold cutting up the meat. If it's not cold enough, meat will tend to be too soft and squishy, making it very difficult to cut. The night before the animal was to be butchered, the "victim" was led into a small barn. One of my brothers would take a 22 gauge rifle and shoot the animal between the eyes. The animal would drop immediately to the floor with a loud clatter. My brothers, on several occasions, tried to get me to shoot the animal, but I always declined. All of my older brothers were great hunters and games-men, but I didn't like killing animals, and still don't to this day. As soon as the cow fell down, Dad was there immediately to slit its throat. The idea was to cut the jugular before the heart quit beating, so all the blood would get drained from the animal.

Shortly thereafter, the belly was slit open, and the entrails removed. It took some time to remove the skin, the hooves, the head, and tail. The hind legs were then tied to a block and tackle, and the animal was hoisted off the floor. Once hanging, the carcass was split right down the middle with a special bone saw (operated with plenty of elbow grease). The two halves were then allowed to hang and cool overnight. It all sounds quite gory and brutal, but it was completely painless to the animal, as her "lights" would go out immediately upon being hit in the brain by the bullet.

My Dad had a rather large "shop" with a pot-bellied stove in it, and we would set up tables inside it to process the meat. Early in the morning, someone would build a fire in the stove, and by eight A.M., it would be warm inside. Butchering was another one of those jobs where all family members were expected to pitch in and help. Two of my bigger brothers would go out to where the beef was hanging, separate, and carry a "quarter beef" at a time into the shop. Knives were soon slicing away, with Dad giving directions as to which part should be cut up for steaks, which part for roasts, and which part for stew beef or hamburger. Most of the "tallow" was cut off and sold, along with the animal skin. By mid-afternoon, the entire animal would be cut up as desired, but the work wasn't done yet.

Mother and my sisters would be busy in the house, canning chunks of beef; usually in two-quart jars. Mother would also take a two-gallon crock and fill it with thin-sliced steaks, heavily salting each layer. The crock was kept in our unheated back porch all winter, and we would have fresh meat from it until close to spring. The pieces of meat set aside for the hamburger had to be ground up that evening, but it had to wait until after the evening chores were done. That often meant it might be eleven P.M. by the time the meat was all processed. My mother made lots of meat balls to can, and canned a great deal of hamburger, as well as freeze a number of packages. Most of our hamburger was pre-seasoned. That is, it had salt and pepper added before it was canned, but the freezer meat was never pre-salted. Mom and Dad rented a freezer box at our local butcher shop in town, where packages of roasts, steaks, and hamburger could be kept all year round, along with poultry, pork, and fruit. We didn't have a freezer at home, and didn't even have a "refrigerator"—just what was called an "ice box." The "ice-man" came around to our house every week, and restocked the ice. Through the very warm weather, we needed a hundred pound block every week. A drip pan was kept underneath the ice-box, and had to be emptied every day. We had to pay the ice-man a whole penny a pound for the blocks of ice.

Sometimes we butchered several pigs at a time, which was an entirely different experience, with making our own sausages, and smoking our own hams and bacon. Then the pig "fat" had to be heated and pressed to make lard. We would often butcher twenty or more chickens, or roosters, at one time, and Mother would can or freeze the meat. My brothers were forever hunting squirrels in the fall, and rabbits in early winter months, not to mention all the fish they would catch, giving Mom plenty of meat and fish to fix for the family throughout the year.

Amish Weddings

An Amish wedding is quite different from what most people would consider a "traditional wedding" in America. Dating usually takes place over a period of years, and when the two decide they both like each other a lot, they will become exclusive, by announcing that they are now "going steady". The going steady period can last as long as two or three years, as the couple saves money to prepare for the purchase of property, and a house to live in. Also, both the boy and the girl are expected to go through counselling by the church elders, and be baptized, before the wedding can take place. If everything goes according to plan, and there is no "break up" during the steady period, a wedding is planned, usually in secret, with only the parents of the couple and perhaps the elders of the church knowing about it. About a month, or six weeks before the wedding, the couple's plans are publicly "announced" before the church, and invitations are sent out to relatives, friends, and the local church congregations of the couple.

There can be as many as three or four hundred people invited, sometimes even more, and preparations have to begin in earnest for such a large gathering. The Amish have no church houses to meet in. Usually a close relative, or one of the parents, will prepare their house, barn, or shed to accommodate the wedding ceremony. Most of the time, the reception, which consists of a large lunch, and an even larger evening dinner, will take place at a different location than where the ceremony is held.

There are always 6 young people directly involved in the wedding party. The couple getting married, along with two other couples as witnesses, called the "nevah huckah" (those who sit beside). Generally, these two couples are not married, are baptized members of the Amish church, and are either close relatives or close friends to those getting married. Beside these two extra couples, about 5 to 8 other young couples have to be selected to serve as table waiters, for the two large meals. A head cook has to be chosen, and a number of assistant cooks secured. The entire meal has to be planned well ahead of time, and the food purchased and prepared. Someone is chosen to make the wedding cake, which can be every bit as elaborate as anything one would purchase or select from a commercial establishment. Fancy napkins, usually bearing the name of the wedding couple and the date of the wedding, are ordered. Sometimes special wine glasses, or fancy decanters, are filled with candy, frills, and specially engraved ornaments, bearing the name of the table waiters and the witnesses, to set on the wedding party table. Dress material is carefully selected, and the bride to be has her mother or older sister make it for her, or she may decide to make it herself. Material is also selected for the dresses of the lady witnesses, and for all the table waiters, so they will be wearing matching dresses.

While the women will be busy preparing all the food, the dresses, and decorations for the tables, the men will be busy preparing the place for the ceremony and the tables for the meals. Usually they will have seating benches that can double as tables by putting them in special brackets, but sometimes they will also make temporary tables completely from scratch, just for the occasion.

The wedding is an all day affair, and will usually start around 9:00 AM. The wedding service and ceremony will last from 2 to 2 1/2 hours. In the last half hour, the actual wedding ceremony will take place, and the couple will say their vows. There is no exchange of rings, and no wedding kiss to complete the ceremony. The couple is just pronounced married, followed by a prayer, and a final closing hymn sung by the congregation. The couple will file out and make their way to the reception place, which usually is somewhere close by in the same neighborhood, but can be as much as a mile or two away. Everyone who was invited for the wedding ceremony is also invited for the lunch, which is a complete meal, with meat, potatoes or dressing, a vegetable, salad or coleslaw, fruit, and desserts: usually pudding, pie, and cake. sometimes ice-cream is served as well. It has been customary to pass a bowl of assorted candy bars around, and everyone can select one. Coffee and water are served as beverages. there can be as many as 8, 10, or more separate tables, and a young dating age couple will be waiting on each one, making sure the bowls of food are never empty, and that everyone has beverages. The food dishes are passed around family style.

The cake is always set up at the head table, in front of where the wedding couple will sit. The witnesses, the parents, and the family of the newlyweds will sit at the head table as well. After lunch, church members will gather around and sing more songs. Later in the afternoon, the couple usually opens their gifts in front of the guests, and thanks each individual personally for the gift they gave. Meanwhile, the cooks and kitchen help will be busy washing dishes and preparing more food for the evening meals. The closest family members; in-laws, aunts, uncles, and friends, will be invited to stay for the evening meal, too, which may be more elaborate than the lunch.

After the adults and younger children have eaten; being waited on by the young couples, the table is again set with clean dishes for another serving. At about 6 PM, the young dating age people will begin to arrive. These might be relatives, friends, or neighboring church members who were invited for the evening. They will form two groups, one of the young lads, the other group of the young ladies. Those who are "going steady" will find their way to the table together, but the dating age "unattached" boys will file past the single girls, and each will choose one to join them in dining. During the young people's dinner, or "supper" as they call it, the older married couples will be waiting on them. After supper is over, the young people will all join in singing songs until 9:00 PM or later.

Finally, the wedding and the feasting is over, and the newlyweds are free to leave the dirty dishes and leftover food for someone else to take care of, while they go to their prearranged place to spend their first night together as husband and wife.

Amish Recreation

Amish youths and adults alike find many ways to amuse themselves without having to have television, video games, and stereo systems. Many a night my brothers, sisters, and I would go out on a moonlit night and play "Who's Afraid of the Big Bad Wolf?" Someone would play the part of the "wolf" and go hide. There was always a "safe haven" where the wolf could not touch you, but the object was to go find the wolf and get back to the safe haven before he could jump out and touch you. Everyone who got touched by the wolf would join the "wolf pack" and go hide again, until there were no more children left to catch. The one that held out the longest would be declared the winner, and be the lone wolf to start the game all over again.

"Kick the Can" is another favorite among Amish children, usually played in the day time. A tin can is set up close to "home base." Everyone goes and hides except for the one that is "it". The "it" person then goes searching for those that are hiding. Whoever he or she finds and touches, must then go and stand on "home base". As the "it" person spreads out farther and farther from home base looking for all who are hiding, one of those hiding might sneak around without being seen, and "kick the can," in which case everyone on home base can run and hide again, provided they don't get touched first. A game called "Whistle, Wink, or Wave" is played in similar fashion, but instead of kicking the can, someone hiding can either "whistle, wink, or wave" at those on base, and if they can hear the whistle, or see the wink, or wave, they are free to go hide again.

Another favorite game is "Dare Base" where two safety lines are formed about 40 to 60 feet apart, with an equal or near equal amount of children behind each line, facing each other. A "base" is made about 5 or 10 feet from each line, where those "captured" are made to stand. Those "caught" by their opponents must stand on their opponent's base. Children behind each line move out toward the center, daring those of the other team to try to capture them. Those first off the line are vulnerable to capture if touched by someone of the opposing team, who has moved off his or her line later. Those "captured" can be freed if someone from their team dashes across the opposing teams safety line without being touched.

Other popular children's games are Tag, Red Rover, Kick Ball, Andy Over, Hide and Seek, Charades, and in the winter time: Fox and Geese. For the older children, Croquette, softball, basketball, and volleyball are popular sports. Many buy ice skates and will take up skating in winter. Besides these, there are many games that dating age Amish play such as "Spin the Bottle", "Drop the Handkerchief", "Pleased or Displeased", "Who, What, and Where", "Telephone", "Treasure Hunt" and "Walk-a-Mile". In Walk-a-Mile, a long row of couples walk down a country road, usually with their arms around each other, with all the young guys on one side, and all the girls on the other side. Usually there is one extra guy, or sometimes an extra couple. The extra guy will walk along side the guys, and find a lady he wants to walk with, whereupon he will tell the guy to move ahead or back 3 or 4 couples (more or less) and he will take his place beside that girl as they go walking. If there is an extra girl, she will be doing the same thing on the side that the girls are on. Only the first one to "butt in" gets to choose who to walk with, and the rest of the walkers have to go where they are told from then on. In "Pleased or Displeased" all the guys and the ladies form a circle, while he who is "it" goes around asking each one in turn "Are you pleased or displeased". If the person is displeased, he or she is asked "What can I do to please you?" The displeased person can then say anything he or she wants to, such as "I want Mary to sit beside John" or "I want Henry and Becky to sing Mary Had a Little Lamb." It is kind of like playing spin the bottle, except all the conditions are thought up as the game progresses.

Another popular party game is "Drop the Blanket" where two teams are chosen or numbered off. One team will be in one room of the house, the other team will be in an adjoining room, with a door in between. Two people will not be a part of the competition, and will stand at the door way on chairs, holding a blanket over the door opening. Each team will then select a boy or girl to stand facing the doorway. The blanket is then dropped, and which ever one standing facing the door names the other first, will win that particular round, and the loser will have to join the winning team. This continues until one team eventually has everyone on their side of the door.

The older and the married Amish are not against having a sporting good time, either. Many continue playing Volleyball and softball up into their 50's and beyond. Others take up horseshoes, checkers, fishing, and hunting. Parker Brother's Rook cards and other card and board games are popular. Putting puzzles together is especially popular with the older generation. Many love to travel, seeing parts of the country, or going on tours. Some will go camping or on fishing trips for a week-end, or even an entire week. There is seldom a dull moment in an Amish household, and for the most part, games and activities involve the whole family, and sometimes the whole neighborhood, or the aunts, uncles, and cousins. The Amish work hard, but they play just as hard, while laughing and having an enjoyable time with both.

Amish "Frolics"

The Amish often have what they call a "frolic" in order to raise a barn, a shed, or even frame in a house for someone in the neighborhood. In such occasions, people of the neighborhood will get together early in the morning, quite often Saturday morning, since many of the younger generation no longer farm, but work in factories or on carpentry crews Monday through Friday. The "frolic" is considered a fun time, and not looked upon as drudgery. Most Amish adults are skilled carpenters, and it is amazing how quickly they can raise a barn or frame in a house. They will gladly donate a day's labor to a neighbor, a relative, a friend, or a brother in the church. In case of fire or storm damage, the Amish have their own form of "insurance" by collecting money within their church congregations to cover most of the damages from such catastrophes.

A date is set for the frolic, and those involved will gather punctually at the designated work area. Crew leaders are established, and the work crews will cooperate as one crew builds and puts the floor down, while other crews are putting together walls, and still others preparing the rafters for when the walls are erected. As soon as the rafters are up, a crew will begin to lay the sheeting on the roof, and another group will come in behind them to put on the shingles. Meanwhile, others are finishing up the interior walls, putting in windows, building stables for the horses, stanchions for the cows, feeding troughs, or whatever else the owner wants in his barn. Some may be doing plumbing, and still others cement work. Each worker contributes his particular skill and know-how to the construction project. The secret to their success lies in their teamwork, cooperation, and coordination.

At noon, the entire crew will take an hour to enjoy a well-prepared meal that the neighborhood wives have been preparing for them. A few minutes of relaxation and jesting after dinner, and they all jump back to work with enthusiasm that would shame most production lines. By evening, the house, barn, or shed, will be framed in and roofed. You would think the structure would have been worked on for weeks.

Making Ice Cream

Ice cream is a favorite dessert among the Amish, as it is for many other people. They will readily buy ice cream from a store, or visit the local Dairy Queen, but they are also very fond of making their own homemade ice cream. Today, they will use crushed ice from a local grocer or quick mart to churn their own, but when I was growing up on the farm, we still had the old ice boxes instead of a regular refrigerator. An ice man would come around once every week to bring us a big block of ice. In the hottest weather, we used an entire 100 pound block, but quite often 25 pounds of that would go toward making homemade ice cream.

Mother would make a gallon of custard out of whole milk, eggs, extra cream, sugar, vanilla, and corn starch. She would pour it into the center canister of the ice cream freezer, and let it cool in the ice box, or in our basement, until late afternoon. My brothers and I would put a 25 pound block of ice into a large burlap feed bag, put it on the ground, and crush the ice by pounding on it with the flat side of an ax. We would then place the canister 3/4 full of custard into the freezer bucket, lock the crank apparatus on top, and pack the crushed ice around the outside of the canister, mixing several pounds of salt in with the ice as we did so. We would then cover the freezer bucket with the burlap bag, and start cranking.

As we took turns cranking the ice cream freezer, the entire canister would rotate in the freezer bucket. Inside the canister there was a "wing" that would constantly stir the ice cream mix, and keep scraping the sides of the canister on the inside, so that the frozen custard would mix with the non-frozen custard. After cranking for about 10 minutes, the custard would start to freeze, and the cranking would keep getting more difficult. Toward the end, 2 or 3 people had to keep relieving each other every few minutes because of the difficulty in turning the crank.

When we thought the ice cream was hard enough, we would take the lid off the canister and remove the wing out of the ice cream. We would place the lid back on, and re-pack ice and salt over the entire freezer. After sitting for another hour or 2, everyone was hungry and ready for ice cream!

Childhood Memories

I still distinctly remember sleeping in a small cradle, under the southwest living room window of our red brick farm house. I remember being handed the bottle there, and being rocked in the cradle by my sisters. I was, in fact, rather jealous of my brother being able to sleep in a crib in Mom and Dad's bedroom, while I slept out in the living room. One rather vivid memory I have as a very young child is going to church at a neighbor's house (Amish take turns hosting their church services in their homes). I was probably only 2 years old at the time, if that, and was sitting beside Dad on a bench after church services were over. Someone brought their one-year old child out and sat him down beside me; he being only a little younger than I was, but still in his diapers. He had nothing on but diapers and rubber pants. I was totally embarrassed, and kept nudging him over closer and closer to the end of the bench, until he finally fell off. I don't think I ever heard anyone scream so loud in my life, and then I felt rather awful at having done such a horrible thing.

I remember Dad rocking me to sleep nearly every night, and when I had outgrown the little cradle, my older brother and I were placed in a small bed at the south east corner of the living room—our bed serving as a couch during the day time. Our mattress, for awhile at least, was a big straw tick, and it took some sleeping on after it was stuffed with fresh straw to wear all the "prickles" down so they wouldn't scratch us at night. An older sister gave me a toy windup train for my third birthday. It didn't need tracks, and it would make "toot toot" sounds going across the floor, with sparks flying out of the wheels. Mom told me to be careful and not wind it too tight, or it might break. I didn't take her too seriously, because I wound it too tight, and broke it.

One day when I was about 5 years old, I went along with one of my older brothers to bring home one of our repaired cultivators from a blacksmith shop. We went with a wagon pulled by a team of horses. On the way home I fell asleep on the wagon floor, so when my brother drove into our driveway rather sharply, I rolled off, and the wagon wheel went over my foot. It just so happened that a Watkins salesman was there at the time, and he immediately had Mom put some ointment of his on my foot. We seldom went to the doctor for such things, except in extreme emergencies.

The bantam roosters and I never got along at home on the farm. For some reason they would chase after me; probably because I was always scared of them. One time one was chasing me, and one of my older brothers threw a rock at it and killed it. Dad got rather upset with him over that. I also had a good reputation in the neighborhood for getting bit by dogs that "never bite anyone". I think they must have sensed my fear, and would come up behind me and bite me in the bottom before I knew what was happening.

One day my next older brother Raymond and I both wanted to go out and have a good look at the bee hives under an apple tree in our backyard orchard. They came after us, and we each got multiple stings. My dad sometimes drove an iron stake into the ground in our apple orchard, so he could chain the bull fast where he would have plenty of grass to eat. Dad would attach the chain to the bull's nose ring, and slip the ring on the other end of the chain over the iron stake. Ray and I went up close to the bull one day when we were still too young to be in school. The bull shook his head up and down, and the chain flew off the iron stake. Ray and I were both too scared to stay around long enough to see what the bull would do, but ran as fast as we could for the house, about a hundred feet away. Luckily, the bull did not realize he wasn't fast to the stake anymore, and went back to eating grass until Dad went back out to slip his chain onto the stake again.

A great pass time of my brothers and I was to tunnel through the straw in our straw shed once it had been completely filled up to the rafters with straw after threshing the wheat and the oats. We always had to wait several weeks, until the straw had settled firm enough so there was little or no danger of it collapsing. We would start digging somewhere close to the top, and burrow our way clear down to the floor, pulling one hand full loose at a time, and shoving the loose straw all the way back up and out the hole where we began the tunnel. This would go on for days until we had a series of tunnels branching off of the main tunnel in several different directions. it was totally dark inside, and we had to feel our way around, but once we got down to the floor boards, there were cracks in the boards just wide enough to allow a faint light to come through. Once the loose straw would get used up, Dad would buy semi-truck loads of bales. We then used the bales to build tunnels, making catacombs by erecting walls 3 and 4 bales high, and putting bales cross wise over the top, so it was completely enclosed and dark inside. Sometimes we would put hideouts inside, or rooms large enough for half a dozen people to sit inside. By the time we were done, we had a maze large enough for our neighbor kids to get lost in. At times we would have to go in and help them find their way out—and sometimes, when I was still quite young, my older brothers would have to come inside and help me find my way out.

When I was 4 or 5 years old, I was chased by a bigger and older Amish boy. I do not know why he started chasing me, perhaps I did something to irritate him. I tried to get away from him, and I remember running down a long gravel or dirt road, or perhaps a lane. He finally caught up with me, tussled me down, and commenced to beat me and pull my hair, whereupon I bit him a good one in the arm or hand. That was the end of that, as he got back up screaming and bawling and ran back and told my mom and dad. I don't know if I was spanked or not, but I do remember that I was the one to get in trouble for being such a terrible boy as to bite someone on the hand.

I also have many positive memories of growing up on the farm, of making maple syrup and apple butter, butchering day, threshing and filling the silo, of putting loose hay in the barn. By the time we were six or seven, Ray and I were already driving the team out in the fields to pick up the loose hay. I know I was out plowing by the time I was in second grade, and helping husk the corn. My early chores in the barn at that time were to bed down the cows and horses with fresh straw. Later, I also had to feed and water the horses, heifers, and calves, and would often help with the milking.

One day I shall never forget, when I was about 10 years old, was my first trip to an area pond where gravel had been dug out. The gravel pit was situated on land owned by several older ladies, who didn't want anyone trespassing on their land, or their pond. LaMar, Ray, and I (the 3 pictured on the front of this book) were sent to the back 10 acres to pull weeds out of the corn field. Instead, Ray and I both piled onto LaMar's bike, and he took us for an excursion to the forbidden "Pit" about a mile and a half southwest of our farm. We put all our clothes except our under shorts behind some bushes up on the bank, though LaMar had actual trunks to wear. We weren't in taking a "dip" very long until we saw someone throw all our clothes into the water way over on the other side of the pit. LaMar, the only one of us who could swim, went over and salvaged what he could—his pants and mine, and Ray's shirt, were the only things he could find. LaMar lost both his shoes (Ray & I had been barefooted). We all snuck home through the corn fields, and made it home without Mom and Dad ever finding out.

I remember some of the daring exploits of my older brothers when I was very young. At one time several of them climbed to the top gable of the barn, and placed a plank across from the top barn window to the top of the silo, daring each other to walk across, which several of them did. We were forever playing tag in the barn, and the braver ones would run across the beams in the barn, some 12 or 15 feet above the floor of the barn.

We had our share of injuries, too. An older brother had two of his fingers taken off by a corn sheller. The same brother also shot himself through the foot with a gun he wasn't supposed to have had, and didn't tell our parents until the following day. He ended up getting blood poisoning, and nearly losing his leg. Another brother lost a finger from an ax. I somersaulted onto a pitchfork in one of our haymows, and had the tine of the fork stuck into my right calf. On another occasion I had a horse kick the handle of a pitchfork into my throat, and I couldn't talk above a whisper for several days. I had a horse reach across his manger and bite me in the chest, through a heavy winter coat, a shirt, and my long-johns, leaving his teeth marks on my skin. A large draft horse kicked both feet out behind him, just touching my chest, but not hurting me. Had I been 6 inches closer, I might have had my rib cage kicked in. There were always dangers present. We must have kept our guardian angels busy, but there are many wonderful and valuable memories woven into my early life, that made it all worthwhile.

Made in United States
North Haven, CT
29 July 2025